THE ESSENCE OF MOTIVATIONAL SPEAKING

INSPIRING CHANGE IN OTHERS

DR. MINAKSHI BANSAL

Made with ♥ on the Notion Press Platform
www.notionpress.com

DEDICATION

This book is dedicated to all who dare to speak and inspire. To the voices that have not yet found their full strength, and to those seasoned speakers who continue to refine their craft with passion and purpose. May you all find the courage to share your stories and the wisdom to touch hearts. This is for the dreamers, the educators, and the leaders of tomorrow. May your words light the way for others, just as your predecessors have lit the way for you.

❥❥❥

Contents

Contents

Prayer

"Om Bhadram Karnebhih Shrinuyama Devah
Bhadram Pashyemakshabhiryajatrah
Sthirairangais Tushtuvamsastanubhih
Vyashema Devahitam Yadayuh
Svasti Na Indro Vriddhashravah
Svasti Nah Pusha Vishwavedah
Svasti Nastarkshyo Arishtanemih
Svasti No Brihaspatir Dadhatu
Om Shantih Shantih Shantih"

This mantra is a prayer for universal well-being, invoking the blessings of various deities for protection, health, and happiness. It emphasizes the importance of experiencing the auspicious through all senses and living a life aligned with divine purpose. The repetition of "Shantih" at the end signifies a deep desire for peace in the individual, the environment, and the universe at large. This mantra is often recited as a prayer for peace, prosperity, and the physical and spiritual well-being of all beings.

ॐॐॐ

About The Author

Dr. Minakshi Bansal, born in the bustling metropolis of Delhi, India, has led a life steeped in artistry, scholarly pursuit, and an unwavering commitment to societal betterment. Following her marriage, she relocated to Ahmedabad, Gujarat, where she has since blossomed into a multifaceted beacon of inspiration for many. Dr. Minakshi is not only recognized as a gifted artist in the realm of Fine Arts but also as an esteemed author, a devoted social worker and a dedicated research scholar in Psychology. Her journey, marked by a profound dedication to elevating those around her, especially the downtrodden and underprivileged children of society, is a testament to her deep-seated belief in the transformative power of engagement and empathy.

From her earliest days, Minakshi was distinguished by an insatiable appetite for reading. Her literary universe was inhabited by characters and narratives that spanned ethical tales, motivational and inspirational stories, and the mythic parables imbued with life lessons. This voracious reading habit was not merely for personal edification but was driven by a desire to distill and disseminate the essence of these narratives to foster the development of students and peers alike. She was particularly captivated by the lives and teachings of historical figures and spiritual leaders such as Adi Shankaracharya, Swami Vivekananda, Dr. APJ Abdul Kalam, Mahamana Pandit Madan Mohan Malviya, Mahatma Gandhi, Sardar Vallabhai Patel, and Vinoba Bhave, among others. Their philosophies and life stories fueled her ambition to embody their ideals of resilience, selflessness, and relentless pursuit of knowledge.

Dr. Minakshi's academic and practical engagement with psychology has been equally noteworthy. As a research scholar, her focus has been on exploring the intricate tapestry of the human psyche, aiming to unlock the potential for psychological well-being and societal harmony. Her scholarly work is complemented by her active involvement in social work, where she employs her academic insights to make tangible differences in the lives of the underprivileged. Her endeavours in social work are characterized by an innovative approach that combines traditional wisdom with contemporary psychological practices to address the multifaceted challenges faced by these communities.

Her artistic talents, another facet of her diverse capabilities, are not merely a personal passion but also serve as a medium through which she communicates and connects with others. Her art, rich in symbolism and emotional depth, reflects her philosophical inquiries and social concerns, offering viewers a glimpse into the breadth of her intellect and the depth of her compassion.

In addition to her contributions to the arts and social sciences, Dr. Minakshi has embraced the healing arts of Pranic Healing, mastering the techniques developed by Master Choa Kok Sui. This practice, which focuses on the manipulation of Prana or life energy to heal the body and aura, has been both a personal journey of discovery and a means through which she extends her healing touch to others. Her proficiency in Pranic Healing is complemented by her advocacy and teaching of various forms of meditation aimed at rejuvenation, personal betterment, and the cultivation of harmony within individuals and communities alike.

Dr. Minakshi's life is a narrative of relentless pursuit, not just of personal achievement but of the upliftment and empowerment of society at large. Her diverse interests and talents—spanning the arts, literature, psychology, and the healing practices—converge on a singular path of service. She embodies the spirit of the luminaries who inspired her, channelling their legacy through her actions and teachings. Through her books, art, and social initiatives, she continues to inspire a new generation to embark on their own journeys of self-discovery, resilience, and altruism.

Her commitment to social betterment, particularly her focus on uplifting underprivileged children, reflects a deep understanding of the transformative potential of education and personal development. By integrating her knowledge of psychology, her artistic sensibilities, and her healing practices, Dr. Bansal has developed a holistic approach to social work that addresses both the immediate needs and the long-term well-being of the communities she serves.

As an author, Dr. Minakshi's writings offer a blend of inspirational insights, practical wisdom, and reflective contemplations drawn from her extensive reading and life experiences. Her books serve as a guide for those seeking to navigate the complexities of life with grace, resilience, and purpose. Through her narratives, she extends an invitation to her readers to explore the depths of their own potential and to contribute meaningfully to the collective well-being of society.

In Dr. Minakshi Bansal, we find a remarkable synthesis of the artist, the scholar, the healer, and the social activist. Her life's work stands as a beacon of hope and a source of inspiration for individuals seeking to make a difference in the world. Her story is a compelling reminder of the power of individual action, rooted in compassion and driven by a profound commitment to the betterment of humanity. Dr. Minakshi's legacy is not just in the tangible outcomes of her efforts but in the enduring spirit of inquiry, empathy, and service that she embodies.

ppp

Preface

This preface aims to set the stage for what you will discover in the pages that follow: a comprehensive guide designed to equip you with the tools, insights, and strategies necessary to become a successful motivational speaker.

Motivational speaking is more than just delivering speeches; it is about connecting with people on a fundamental level and using words to ignite transformation. Whether you are speaking to a small group or addressing thousands, the essence of effective motivational speaking lies in your ability to communicate messages that resonate with your audience and compel them to act or change their perspective.

The intent of this book is not merely to provide you with technical skills for better speaking but to delve deeper into the subtleties that make a speaker truly impactful. From understanding your audience's core needs to expressing genuine empathy, and from harnessing your personal stories to leveraging your unique voice, this book covers the gamut of essentials that define a powerful speaker.

As we begin, it's important to recognize that every motivational speaker embarks on a personal journey that is as unique as their background and experiences. This book is crafted to be your companion throughout your own journey in motivational speaking, offering guidance that is broad in scope yet detailed enough to foster deep understanding and application.

You might be at the outset of your speaking career, looking to find your voice and develop your initial presentations, or you might be an experienced speaker seeking to refine your skills and reach larger audiences. Regardless of where you stand today, the principles and practices outlined here are designed to be universally applicable, providing value whether you are addressing a community gathering or a global conference.

This guide is structured to walk you through every aspect of motivational speaking. It begins by helping you understand the critical importance of knowing and connecting with your audience. This foundational knowledge sets the stage for subsequent chapters that explore how to craft your message with clarity and how to deliver it with power and authenticity.

As you progress, you'll learn about the nuances of body language, the dynamics of audience interaction, and the effective use of humor to enhance engagement. Additionally, you'll discover the significance of preparation and practice—elements that many overlook but are crucial for success.

The latter sections of the book delve into advanced topics such as adapting to different speaking contexts, continuous learning and improvement, and finally, building and maintaining a personal brand that resonates with your target audience. These sections are designed to provide a roadmap for sustained growth and success, enabling you to continue evolving as a speaker and influencer.

Throughout the book, you will find practical advice and actionable tips that you can implement immediately. These include strategies for dealing with nervousness, engaging disinterested audiences, and handling unexpected situations during speeches. Moreover, the book is enriched with inspirational case studies from well-known motivational speakers, offering you a glimpse into the journeys of those who have excelled in this field.

As the author, my hope is that this book serves not just as a manual for becoming a motivational speaker but as a source of inspiration that encourages you to pursue excellence in every speech you deliver. The journey of becoming a motivational speaker is as rewarding as it is challenging, filled with opportunities for personal growth and the profound satisfaction of impacting lives positively.

So, whether your aim is to inspire students, uplift corporate teams, or lead community changes, the insights contained in this book are your stepping stones to becoming a speaker who not only talks the talk but truly walks the walk.

Thank you for choosing this book as your guide. I look forward to being part of your journey in mastering the art of motivational speaking and witnessing the incredible impacts you will make. Let's begin this transformative journey together.

ppp

ONE

INTRODUCTION TO MOTIVATIONAL SPEAKING

Motivational speaking is a special type of public speaking where the main goal is to inspire and motivate people to make positive changes in their lives. It is a powerful tool because it can influence how people think and feel, encouraging them to take action toward achieving their goals. This form of speaking is not just about delivering speeches; it's about connecting with an audience on a deep level and helping them see new possibilities for themselves.

The essence of motivational speaking lies in its ability to reach into the hearts and minds of listeners. When a motivational speaker talks, they do more than just share information. They create an experience that can leave a lasting impact. They use words to paint pictures of better futures, to stir emotions, and to awaken desires that drive people to move forward. This is why many find motivational speaking so captivating; it offers a spark of hope and inspiration.

One of the main reasons motivational speaking is so effective is that it appeals to our universal desire for growth and improvement. Everyone, at some point in their lives, feels the need to change or enhance some aspect of their life, whether it's personal or professional. A motivational speaker helps to ignite that desire by providing not just the vision but also the energy to start making those changes. They make the path to improvement seem attainable and worth pursuing.

Another key aspect of motivational speaking is empathy. A good motivational speaker understands the feelings and challenges of their audience. They can empathize with their struggles, which helps in establishing a strong connection. This empathy is crucial because it makes the audience feel understood and supported, which is often what people need to be motivated.

Storytelling is another powerful tool used in motivational speaking. Stories are not just entertaining; they are also incredibly persuasive. By sharing personal anecdotes or the success stories of others, speakers can illustrate their points in ways that facts and statistics cannot. Stories make the message relatable and memorable. They allow the speaker to demonstrate the transformation they are advocating for, making it more tangible for the audience.

Authenticity is equally important in motivational speaking. People can usually tell when someone is being genuine or just putting on an act. When a speaker is authentic, their message carries more weight. The audience is more likely to trust and believe in the speaker, which increases the impact of the message. Authenticity builds trust and rapport, which are essential for any speaker looking to motivate others.

Motivational speakers also need to overcome their fears. Public speaking is one of the most common fears people have, and even experienced speakers can feel nervous. However, overcoming this fear is part of what makes a motivational speaker effective. It shows the audience that it's possible to face and conquer one's fears, which is a powerful motivational message in itself.

Additionally, motivational speaking is not a one-size-fits-all approach. Each speech must be tailored to the specific audience and setting. A speaker must consider the unique characteristics and needs of their audience and adjust their message accordingly. This customization makes the speech more relevant and more likely to resonate with listeners.

The power of motivational speaking also lies in its ability to evoke action. A successful motivational speech doesn't just make people feel good; it inspires them to take action. This could be as simple as changing a daily habit, or as significant as making a major life decision. The true measure of a motivational speaker's success is the change they inspire in their audience.

In conclusion, motivational speaking is a unique and powerful form of communication that has the ability to inspire change and positively influence lives. It combines empathy, storytelling, authenticity, and a deep understanding of the audience to deliver messages that motivate. Through their speeches, motivational speakers not only share knowledge but also encourage and empower their listeners to achieve more than they thought was possible. This is what makes motivational speaking an essential tool for inspiring change and fostering growth in individuals and communities alike.

ppp

Understanding Your Audience: "To truly speak to someone, you must first understand their world. Great speakers listen with the mind and see with the heart. They craft messages not just to the ears but to the soul. Knowing your audience is the first step to moving them towards action. Speak not only to be heard, but to touch lives."

TWO
KNOWING YOUR AUDIENCE

Understanding your audience is a crucial part of motivational speaking. It's the key to delivering messages that not only reach the ears of listeners but also resonate with their hearts and minds. To truly influence people, a speaker must first know who they are speaking to. This involves more than just recognizing faces in a crowd. It's about understanding their backgrounds, their current situations, and what they hope to gain from listening to you.

The first step in knowing your audience is to gather information about them. This might involve researching the demographic characteristics of the audience, such as age, gender, profession, and educational background. Such details can give insights into the interests, challenges, and aspirations of the audience. For example, speaking to a group of university students about career planning will differ significantly from speaking to retirees interested in leisure and travel.

Another important aspect is understanding the cultural and social context of your audience. Different cultures have different values, beliefs, and practices. A message that resonates well with an audience in one cultural setting might not work in another.

Therefore, it's important for motivational speakers to be culturally sensitive and tailor their messages to align with the cultural context of their audience.

Once you have a general understanding of who your audience is, the next step is to dive deeper into their specific needs and expectations. Why are they attending your speech? What are they hoping to learn or gain from it? Some might look for motivation to overcome personal challenges, while others might seek practical advice or inspiration for professional growth. Knowing this can help you structure your speech to address these needs directly.

To further refine your understanding of your audience, consider their emotional and psychological states. People come into a motivational speech with various emotions—some may be skeptical, others might be hopeful, and some could be indifferent. Recognizing these emotional states can help you connect more effectively. For instance, if you sense skepticism, you might use more evidence and real-life success stories to back up your points. On the other hand, if the audience is hopeful, you might focus on uplifting and visionary content.

Engaging with your audience before the speech can also provide valuable insights. This could be through informal conversations, surveys, or interactive social media posts. Such interactions can reveal what your audience is most interested in or concerned about. They also show that you care about their views and are there to address their specific needs, which can build rapport and trust even before you step onto the stage.

During the speech, observing audience reactions is crucial. Are they nodding in agreement, or do they look confused? Are they checking their phones, or are they leaning forward, engaged? Such cues can tell you a lot about whether your message is hitting the mark or if adjustments are needed. Experienced speakers often adjust their delivery on the fly based on these reactions, which is a skill that comes with practice and attentiveness.

Feedback after the event is equally important. Encouraging feedback, whether through formal questionnaires or casual conversations, can provide insights into what worked well and what didn't. This feedback is invaluable for improving future speeches and further understanding your audience.

Knowing your audience is about much more than just facing a group of people. It's about understanding their backgrounds, cultures, needs, and emotional states. It requires research, empathy, and adaptability. By truly understanding your audience, you can craft messages that not only inform but also inspire and motivate. This is what makes the difference between a speech that is merely heard and one that sparks change.

❧❧❧

The Power of Empathy: "Empathy bridges the gap between knowing and feeling. It transforms speeches from monologues into dialogues. When you speak with empathy, you speak to one heart at a time. The true power of communication lies in not just sharing your thoughts but feeling the thoughts of others. Connect deeply, and the impact will follow."

❤❤❤

THREE

THE POWER OF EMPATHY

Empathy is often described as the ability to put oneself in another person's shoes. In the context of motivational speaking, empathy is not just a nice-to-have quality; it is an essential tool that enables speakers to connect deeply with their audience, fostering a sense of understanding and trust that can significantly enhance the impact of the message being delivered.

Empathy in motivational speaking involves more than just feeling what your audience feels. It is about actively understanding and addressing the emotions, needs, and aspirations of those listening. When a speaker manages to effectively convey empathy, the audience is more likely to open up, engage, and be influenced by the speech. This deep connection can make the difference between a speech that is forgotten as soon as it ends and one that resonates and inspires long-term change.

One of the key benefits of empathy is that it helps to break down barriers. Often, people come into a speech with their defenses up. They might be skeptical or reluctant to fully engage with the message. However, when they sense that the speaker genuinely understands and cares about their experiences and feelings, they are more likely to let down their guard and listen more openly. This creates a fertile ground for the speaker's message to take root.

Empathy also aids in tailoring the message to the specific needs and circumstances of the audience. By understanding what the audience is going through, a speaker can adjust their tone, content, and delivery to better align with the audience's current emotional and situational context. For example, a speaker talking to a group of recent graduates will likely strike a different tone than when speaking to senior executives. Similarly, addressing an audience in a region recently affected by economic downturns would require a different approach compared to an audience in a prosperous area.

To develop and convey empathy, a motivational speaker must first do their homework. This involves researching the audience beforehand—learning about their backgrounds, the challenges they face, and what they care about. This preparation not only equips the speaker with the information needed to connect but also demonstrates to the audience that the speaker has taken the time to understand them, which can build credibility and trust.

Listening is another critical aspect of empathy. While a motivational speech might seem mostly about talking, effective speakers listen to their audiences, even during a speech. This can be through direct interaction, such as asking questions and encouraging responses, or by reading body language and adjusting the speech in response to the audience's reactions. Good speakers are attentive and responsive, not just delivering a pre-planned script but engaging in a dynamic exchange with their audience.

Sharing personal stories is another powerful way to demonstrate empathy. When speakers share their own experiences, especially struggles and vulnerabilities, it humanizes them and makes them more relatable. It shows the audience that the speaker knows what it's like to face challenges, making the speaker's successes and positive messages more credible and inspiring. Personal stories can bridge the gap between the speaker and the audience, making the messages more personal and impactful.

Empathy extends beyond the speech itself. It involves follow-up after the event, addressing any further questions or discussions that may arise. It shows that the speaker cares about the impact of their words and is committed to supporting their audience beyond the confines of the speech event.

The power of empathy in motivational speaking cannot be overstated. It is what transforms a good speech into an impactful one. By understanding and genuinely caring about the audience's needs and experiences, a speaker can create a powerful connection that enhances the delivery and reception of their message. This connection not only makes the speech more effective but also leaves a lasting impression that can inspire and motivate audiences to take action and embrace change.

Crafting Your Message: "Clarity in speech reflects clarity in thought. A well-crafted message is the heartbeat of effective communication. Simplify the complex—this is the speaker's true art. Every word should serve your message, and every message should serve your audience. Speak to inform, inspire, and ignite."

❦❦❦

CRAFTING YOUR MESSAGE

Creating a clear and impactful message is at the heart of effective motivational speaking. When crafting your message, the goal is to make it so resonant and persuasive that it not only captures the attention of your audience but also inspires them to take action. A well-crafted message can change minds, influence behavior, and inspire people to achieve their highest potential. Here's how you can ensure that the messages you deliver are both clear and impactful.

First and foremost, clarity in your message is crucial. A clear message is easy to understand and free from confusion or ambiguity. To achieve this, start by defining the core idea you want to communicate. This idea should be simple and focused. Avoid trying to cover too many topics or ideas in a single speech. Instead, concentrate on one main theme and build your message around it. This will help your audience grasp your point more effectively and remember it long after your speech is over.

Once you have a core idea, structure your message in a way that logically progresses from start to finish. A well-structured speech typically includes an introduction, a body, and a conclusion. The introduction should hook the audience, the body provides the main content and supporting details, and the conclusion reinforces the main idea and encourages action. This structure not only helps in maintaining clarity but also aids in keeping the audience engaged throughout the speech.

Language plays a significant role in the clarity of your message. Use simple and direct language that can be easily understood by your audience. Avoid jargon, technical terms, or complex phrases that might confuse listeners who are not familiar with that specific vocabulary. The use of vivid and relatable examples can also help clarify complex ideas and ensure that your message is more memorable.

To make your message impactful, it needs to resonate on an emotional level with your audience. Emotions drive action, and by tapping into the emotions of your listeners, you can make your message more persuasive. Use stories, anecdotes, and examples that evoke emotions such as joy, hope, excitement, or even fear and anger, depending on the context and the action you want to inspire. These stories should be relevant to the core message and should help illustrate your points in a way that facts and figures alone cannot.

Another key to crafting an impactful message is relevance. Your message should be relevant to the interests, needs, and challenges of your audience. Before preparing your speech, take time to understand who your audience is and what matters to them. This understanding will allow you to tailor your message in a way that connects directly to their lives and experiences. When an audience feels that a message speaks directly to them, they are more likely to engage with it and take it to heart.

In addition to relevance, your message should also include a clear call to action. Tell your audience exactly what you would like them to do after listening to your speech. Whether it's changing a behavior, pursuing a goal, or simply adopting a new perspective, your call to action should be clear and achievable. A strong call to action turns your message from mere information into a compelling directive that prompts action.

Finally, practice delivering your message before the actual event. Practice helps you refine your language, perfect your delivery, and ensure that your message is as clear and impactful as possible. It also helps you become more confident in your speaking, which in turn makes your message more persuasive.

In crafting your message, remember that the most powerful speeches are those that are clear, resonate emotionally, are relevant to the audience, and include a compelling call to action. By focusing on these elements, you can ensure that your message not only reaches the ears of your listeners but also moves them to action. This is the essence of successful motivational speaking.

ᐅᐅᐅ

Storytelling Techniques: "Stories are the currency of human connection. They carry the power to transport audiences to new worlds and offer new perspectives. A good story told well can captivate the mind and capture the heart. Remember, people may forget what you said, but they will never forget how you made them feel with your story. Let your narrative weave the thread that connects you to your audience."

▷▷▷

FIVE

STORYTELLING TECHNIQUES

Storytelling is one of the most powerful techniques in motivational speaking. A good story can captivate an audience, make complex ideas easier to understand, and embed messages deeply into the memory of listeners. When stories are effectively integrated into speeches, they can transform the delivery from merely informative to profoundly impactful. Here's how you can use storytelling techniques to enhance your speeches and make them more engaging and memorable.

First, it's important to understand why stories work so well. Humans are naturally drawn to narratives. We see our lives and experiences as a series of interconnected events, which is why we relate so easily to stories. Stories evoke emotions and can connect with listeners on a personal level. When you tell a story, you are not just transmitting information, you are creating an experience for your audience.

To begin using stories in your speeches, you should start with selecting the right story. The best stories are those that are relevant to the theme of your speech and resonate with your audience. Think about what you want your audience to feel, think, or do after your speech. Then, choose a story that illustrates your main points in a way that aligns with these objectives. This could be a personal anecdote, a historical event, or even a fictional tale, as long as it supports your message.

Once you have chosen a story, you need to craft it in a way that maximizes its impact. A good story has a clear structure – a beginning, middle, and end. It should have a setting, characters, a conflict, and a resolution. Begin by setting the scene and introducing the characters in a way that your audience can quickly grasp. Then, build up to a conflict or challenge that keeps the listeners engaged, leading to a resolution that ties back to the main message of your speech.

To make your stories more engaging, use vivid details. Descriptive language that appeals to the senses can help your audience visualize the story and feel more connected to it. However, be careful not to overload your story with excessive details that might detract from the main points you are trying to make.

Another effective technique is to make your audience a part of the story. This can be done by asking rhetorical questions that prompt them to think or by relating the story to common experiences that many people share. This inclusion helps the audience relate more personally to the narrative, increasing their interest and engagement.

Remember also to practice the delivery of your story. The way you tell the story can be just as important as the story itself. Use changes in tone, pace, and volume to highlight different parts of the story. Pause to allow key points to resonate with the audience. Your facial expressions, gestures, and body language can also add to the emotional impact of the story.

It is also effective to use stories to evoke specific emotions that are conducive to your message. For example, if you want to inspire your audience to overcome challenges, you might tell a story about someone who faced significant obstacles and triumphed. If you want to underscore the importance of teamwork, you might choose a story that illustrates how people working together can achieve more than they could alone.

Finally, it's important to connect the story back to your overall message. After telling your story, explicitly link it to the main points of your speech. This helps ensure that the story reinforces your message rather than distracting from it.

Storytelling is a vital skill for motivational speakers. Effective stories can engage the audience's emotions, make your message more memorable, and even inspire change. By carefully selecting stories, crafting them well, and delivering them effectively, you can greatly enhance the impact of your speeches and leave a lasting impression on your audience.

ᗡᗡᗡ

Authenticity in Speaking: "Authenticity is your greatest asset. Speak your truth, and it will resonate. The most powerful speeches come from a place of sincerity and genuine passion. When you are real, your audience can feel it—an authentic voice is louder than any microphone. Be yourself; everyone else is already taken."

❦❦❦

SIX

AUTHENTICITY IN SPEAKING

Authenticity in speaking is one of the most critical factors in the effectiveness and impact of a motivational speech. Being genuine helps to establish a connection with the audience that is rooted in trust and relatability. When speakers are authentic, their messages resonate more deeply and inspire greater confidence and motivation among their listeners. Understanding the importance of authenticity and learning how to maintain it can significantly enhance the power of your speeches.

Authenticity means being true to oneself and reflecting genuine beliefs and feelings in your speech. It involves honesty and transparency in what you say and how you say it. An authentic speaker does not put on an act or try to be someone they are not; instead, they share their true self with the audience. This honesty can create a powerful bond between the speaker and the audience because people are naturally drawn to authenticity and can usually tell when someone is being sincere.

The importance of being genuine cannot be overstated. When speakers are authentic, audiences are more likely to trust them. Trust is fundamental in motivational speaking because it encourages listeners to open up and be receptive to the message being shared. Without trust, even the most well-crafted messages can fall flat. Authenticity also fosters a sense of respect and admiration, which can enhance the speaker's credibility and influence.

Maintaining authenticity in speaking starts with self-awareness. Knowing who you are, what you stand for, and what you truly believe is the foundation of authenticity. Before you can be genuine with others, you must be honest with yourself. This involves reflecting on your values, experiences, and motivations. Understanding these elements of your identity allows you to convey your true self to your audience confidently and comfortably.

It is also essential to align your message with your values and beliefs. When preparing your speech, make sure that what you are saying is something you genuinely believe in. If there is a misalignment between your message and your personal beliefs, it can undermine your authenticity and weaken your impact as a speaker. Consistency in your words and actions reinforces authenticity, enhancing your overall effectiveness.

Another key aspect of maintaining authenticity is vulnerability. Sharing your own struggles, failures, and uncertainties can make you more relatable and approachable. It shows the audience that you are human and that you face challenges just like they do. This level of openness can deepen the emotional connection with the audience, making your message more impactful.

However, being vulnerable doesn't mean oversharing or turning the speech into a personal therapy session. It means selecting personal stories and insights that have relevance to your message and that will resonate with your audience. The goal is to strike a balance where your openness serves to illustrate your points and encourage others, not to overshadow the message itself.

Language and delivery also play crucial roles in authenticity. Use your natural speaking style instead of adopting a persona that you think a speaker should have. If you are naturally humorous, let that come through in your speech. If you are more serious, use that to convey depth and sincerity. The key is to be consistent with who you are. Additionally, avoid using jargon or overly complex language that doesn't feel natural to you, as this can make your speech seem forced.

Listening to feedback is another important aspect of maintaining authenticity. Pay attention to how your audience responds to different parts of your speech. Feedback, whether it's verbal or non-verbal, can provide insights into whether your authenticity is resonating with the audience. Use this feedback to adjust and improve your approach.

Authenticity is a cornerstone of effective motivational speaking. Being genuine not only helps to build trust and respect but also enhances the connection and engagement of your audience. By being self-aware, aligning your message with your true beliefs, showing vulnerability, maintaining a natural speaking style, and listening to feedback, you can ensure that your authenticity shines through in every speech. This not only makes your messages more persuasive and inspiring but also leaves a lasting impact on your audience.

ÞÞÞ

Building Confidence: "Confidence in speaking comes from preparation, not just talent. The more you know your material, the more your confidence will grow. Stand in your knowledge, and your voice will follow. Confidence is contagious; it can inspire your audience to believe in your message as much as you do. Speak because you know it's worth hearing."

▷▷▷

SEVEN

BUILDING CONFIDENCE

Building confidence is essential for any motivational speaker. Whether you're addressing a small group or a large audience, the ability to deliver your message with confidence can significantly impact your effectiveness. Confidence not only enhances your credibility but also makes your presentation more engaging and convincing. Fortunately, confidence is a skill that can be developed over time through practice and the right strategies.

One of the most fundamental ways to build confidence is through thorough preparation. Knowing your material well is the first step to feeling confident about delivering it. Spend ample time preparing your speech, understanding your topic deeply, and organizing your thoughts logically. When you feel prepared, it reduces anxiety and boosts your confidence because you know what you are talking about and are less likely to be thrown off by unexpected questions or reactions.

Practicing your speech is another crucial step. Rehearse your speech several times in a setting that is similar to the one you will be speaking in. You can practice in front of a mirror, record yourself, or gather a small audience of friends or family to perform in front of. Pay attention to not just what you are saying but how you are saying it. Work on your voice modulation, pace, and body language. The more you practice, the more natural your delivery will become, which in turn will boost your confidence.

Familiarity with the venue can also help alleviate nervousness. If possible, visit the place where you will be speaking before the event. Get a feel for the space, test any equipment you will be using, and plan out where you will stand and how you will move around during your speech. Being familiar with your environment can reduce anxiety and increase your confidence.

Another effective strategy is to develop a pre-speech routine. This could involve exercises that calm your mind and body, such as deep breathing, stretching, or visualization techniques. Visualizing a successful speech can be particularly powerful. Imagine yourself speaking clearly, engaging your audience, and receiving a positive response. This mental rehearsal can enhance your confidence significantly.

During your speech, maintaining a positive mindset is key. It's normal to feel some nerves, but try to focus on your message and the reason you are there. Remind yourself of your preparation and your desire to share something valuable with your audience. Turning your attention away from yourself and onto your message and your audience can reduce feelings of self-consciousness and bolster your confidence.

Engaging your audience can also enhance your confidence as you speak. Start with a question or a quick interactive activity to break the ice and create a connection with your audience. Seeing your audience react positively can give you a boost of confidence. Additionally, try to make eye contact with different people in the audience throughout your speech. This not only helps in making your delivery more personal but also gets you affirmative nods and smiles that can reassure and encourage you.

Receiving feedback is also a crucial part of building confidence. After your speeches, seek feedback from trusted colleagues, mentors, or audience members. Constructive feedback can provide insights into your strengths and areas for improvement. Knowing what you are doing well can boost your confidence, while understanding your weak points can guide your efforts to improve.

Lastly, embrace any feelings of nervousness as a natural part of the process. Even the most experienced speakers feel nervous. Instead of fighting these feelings, acknowledge them and channel them into energy for your presentation. Often, nerves can actually enhance your performance by keeping you alert and energetic.

Building confidence as a speaker is a journey that involves preparation, practice, and positivity. By thoroughly preparing, practicing your delivery, familiarizing yourself with the venue, maintaining a positive mindset, engaging with your audience, seeking feedback, and embracing your nerves, you can develop the confidence that will make your speeches more effective and impactful. Confidence is not just about feeling good; it's about able to deliver your message in the most compelling way possible.

ᐳᐳᐳ

Overcoming Public Speaking Fears: "Fear is a reaction; confidence is a decision. Face your fears with every speech, and turn your stage into a place of triumph. Remember, the butterflies in your stomach are there to give you wings. Let your passion drown out your fears. Speak not to avoid fear, but to overcome it."

▷▷▷

EIGHT

OVERCOMING PUBLIC SPEAKING FEARS

Overcoming public speaking fears, commonly known as stage fright, is a challenge many people face. The fear of standing in front of an audience and delivering a speech can be daunting. However, with the right strategies, anyone can conquer this fear and become a confident speaker.

The first step in overcoming public speaking fears is to understand the root of your anxiety. Often, fear of public speaking stems from a fear of judgment or making a mistake in front of others. Recognizing what specifically worries you about speaking in public can help you address these fears directly.

Preparation is a critical element in reducing public speaking anxiety. Knowing your material well gives you a foundation of confidence. Spend adequate time preparing your content, organizing your thoughts, and understanding the key points you need to convey. Being well-prepared not only makes you feel more confident but also reduces the likelihood of unexpected issues during your speech.

Practicing your speech multiple times before the actual event is another vital strategy. Practice in front of a mirror, record yourself, or have a rehearsal in front of friends or family. Each practice session should mimic the actual speaking conditions as closely as possible. Focus on your delivery as well as your content, including your voice modulation, pacing, and body language. The more familiar you are with your speech, the less room there is for anxiety to creep in.

Familiarizing yourself with the venue can also lessen anxiety. Visit the location where you will be speaking beforehand if possible. Walk around the stage, test any audio-visual equipment you will be using, and get a feel for the environment. Knowing the layout of the room and what to expect can help ease nerves.

Another effective technique is to visualize success. Imagine delivering your speech confidently and successfully. Visualization is a powerful mental exercise used by professional athletes and public speakers alike. It can help reinforce a positive outcome and decrease fear.

On the day of the speech, manage your physical responses to anxiety through deep breathing or meditation. These techniques can help calm your mind and reduce physical symptoms of nervousness like a racing heart or shaking hands. Practicing these calming methods regularly can make them more effective when you really need them.

When it's time to speak, try to connect with your audience early in the presentation. Starting with a question or an interesting anecdote can engage your audience right away and help you feel more at ease. Making eye contact and seeing nodding heads or smiling faces can boost your confidence and reduce feelings of isolation on stage.

It's also important to accept that some nervousness is normal. Even seasoned speakers get nervous. Instead of fighting your anxiety, acknowledge it as a natural feeling that can actually enhance your performance by keeping you alert and focused.

Lastly, seek opportunities to speak in public regularly. Like any skill, public speaking improves with practice. Joining a group like Toastmasters, a club where people practice public speaking, can provide a supportive environment to build your skills and confidence.

Overcoming public speaking fears is a process that involves preparation, practice, and exposure. By understanding your fears, preparing thoroughly, practicing your delivery, familiarizing yourself with the venue, using visualization and relaxation techniques, engaging with your audience, accepting some level of nervousness, and seeking regular speaking opportunities, you can build your confidence and reduce your anxiety. Public speaking is a powerful skill, and conquering your fears will allow you to share your ideas and stories with confidence.

▷▷▷

Using Visual Aids: "Visual aids are not crutches but catalysts in communication. They can clarify, enhance, and emphasize your message. Use visuals to create a picture that words alone cannot paint. Remember, a picture is worth a thousand words, but the right picture with the right words is priceless. Choose visuals that speak even when you don't."

⊳⊳⊳

NINE

USING VISUAL AIDS

Using visual aids effectively can significantly enhance the impact of a speech. Visual aids such as slides, videos, charts, and graphs can help to clarify points, emphasize key messages, and maintain audience engagement. However, to ensure that these tools are beneficial rather than distracting, it's crucial to use them wisely.

Visual aids should support and complement your speech, not overshadow or replace it. The first step in using visual aids effectively is to plan when and how to use them. This planning should be integrated into the early stages of preparing your presentation. Decide what the main points of your speech are and think about how visual aids could help illustrate these points. This could involve using a chart to show statistical data, a video to provide a real-life example, or a simple graphic to break down complex information into understandable parts.

When creating slides, keep them clear and uncluttered. Each slide should convey only one main idea. Avoid filling slides with too much text; aim for concise bullet points or short, clear statements. The text should be large enough to be easily readable from the back of the room. For consistency and visual appeal, use the same or similar fonts, colors, and styles throughout your presentation. This uniformity helps keep the audience focused on the content rather than being distracted by the design elements.

Images and graphics can be very effective in making your presentation more engaging. However, make sure that every image serves a purpose. Each should reinforce or illustrate the point you're making. Random or irrelevant images can confuse the audience, detracting from the message you're trying to convey.

Videos can be particularly powerful in a presentation, but they come with their own set of challenges. Ensure that any video you plan to show is short, to the point, and directly relevant to your topic. A long or only tangentially related video can cause your audience to lose focus. Additionally, always test video playback in the venue beforehand to avoid technical issues that could interrupt your presentation and undermine your credibility.

Another important aspect of using visual aids is to make sure they are accessible to all audience members. This includes considering people who might have disabilities such as vision or hearing impairments. For instance, provide descriptions for images or diagrams for those who cannot see them and ensure that any videos are subtitled so that everyone can understand them regardless of hearing ability.

During your speech, how you reference your visual aids is as important as their content. Point to the visual aids when you discuss them, and give the audience a moment to absorb the information. This helps to ensure that the visual aids are integrated smoothly into your presentation rather than seeming like an afterthought.

It's also vital to be prepared to speak without your visual aids in case of technical difficulties. Always have a backup plan, such as printed copies of your slides or notes that outline your main points. This preparation ensures that you can continue your presentation smoothly, even if the unexpected happens.

Finally, practice your speech with your visual aids. This practice should mimic the actual speaking conditions as closely as possible. By practicing, you'll be able to ensure that the timing of the visual elements aligns with your spoken words. It will also give you a chance to refine how you transition between speaking and showing the visual aids, which can help maintain the flow of your presentation.

Visual aids can significantly enhance a speech by making it more engaging and helping to clarify and emphasize your points. However, their effectiveness depends on careful planning, design, and integration into your presentation. By following these guidelines, you can ensure that your use of visual aids adds value to your speeches and helps to keep your audience engaged and informed.

ᗺᗺᗺ

Vocal Techniques: "Your voice is an instrument; tune it to the heart of your audience. Variation in tone can keep your speech alive and pulsating. Speak clearly, project loudly and modulate wisely. Let your voice carry not just your words, but your emotions. The way you say something can be just as important as what you say."

ᐅᐅᐅ

TEN

VOCAL TECHNIQUES

Improving vocal techniques is essential for any speaker who wishes to communicate effectively and persuasively. The voice is not just a medium to convey information; it is also a powerful tool that can influence how the message is received and interpreted by the audience. Mastery of vocal techniques can enhance the clarity of your speech, maintain audience interest, and strengthen the persuasive power of your message. Here are some practical techniques to improve your voice for clarity and persuasion.

The first step to enhancing your vocal technique is to ensure clarity in your speech. Clarity involves articulating words clearly so that each word can be easily understood by the audience. This requires conscious effort, especially in public speaking situations where nerves might cause you to mumble or speak too quickly. You can improve your articulation through tongue twisters and reading aloud, focusing on enunciating each syllable. Regular practice of these exercises can help train your mouth and tongue to pronounce words more clearly.

Another important aspect of vocal technique is the control of volume. Your voice should be loud enough to be heard by everyone in the room without straining their ears. However, varying your volume can also be used strategically to emphasize key points or to draw the audience's attention back to your speech if their minds have wandered. For instance, lowering your voice to a near whisper can compel your audience to listen closely, while raising your volume can energize and excite them.

The pitch of your voice also plays a significant role in how your message is received. A monotonous voice can be dull and can lead to disengagement. To keep the audience engaged, vary your pitch throughout your speech. Use a higher pitch to convey excitement or importance and a lower pitch to convey seriousness or caution. Be careful not to overuse any particular pitch to avoid sounding unnatural.

Pacing is another crucial element of effective vocal delivery. The right pace helps your audience to absorb the information you are presenting. Speaking too fast can overwhelm listeners, while speaking too slowly can bore them. Practice finding a comfortable speed that allows for clarity and comprehension. Additionally, incorporating pauses into your speech can provide emphasis and give your audience time to reflect on important points.

Breathing techniques are also vital for effective speaking. Good breath control can help you maintain a steady, clear voice and prevent you from running out of breath. Practice deep breathing exercises to increase your lung capacity and learn to breathe from your diaphragm instead of your chest. This type of breathing supports stronger and more stable vocalization. Before you speak, take a few deep breaths to calm your nerves and center yourself.

To further refine your vocal delivery, consider the emotional tone of your speech. Your voice should reflect the emotions that you want to evoke in your audience. For example, warmth and friendliness can be conveyed through a softer, more melodic tone, while urgency or excitement can be communicated through a brisk and vibrant tone. Being aware of the emotional undertones of your words and matching your vocal delivery to those emotions can significantly enhance the persuasive power of your speech.

Recording your speeches and listening to the playback is an excellent way to evaluate and improve your vocal techniques. Pay attention to your articulation, volume, pitch, pace, and emotional tone. Listening critically to your own recordings can reveal habits such as filler words, monotony, or any other areas that need improvement.

Mastering vocal techniques is crucial for effective and persuasive public speaking. By focusing on articulation, volume, pitch, pace, breathing, and emotional tone, you can enhance the clarity and impact of your speech. Regular practice and self-evaluation are key to developing these skills. With commitment and attention to these aspects of vocal delivery, you can ensure that your voice is a powerful tool in your public speaking arsenal.

ppp

Body Language Basics: "Your body speaks before you do. Align your body language with your message to add depth to your words. A confident stance and purposeful gestures can greatly strengthen your speech's impact. Communicate not just with your words but with every move you make. Let your presence speak volumes."

❦❦❦

ELEVEN

BODY LANGUAGE BASICS

Body language is a crucial aspect of communication, especially in the context of public speaking. Your gestures, facial expressions, and overall posture can significantly reinforce your message, convey confidence, and help engage your audience. Understanding and mastering the basics of body language can make your speeches more compelling and impactful.

First and foremost, it is important to understand that body language speaks volumes about your confidence and attitude towards the subject you are discussing. When you stand upright with your shoulders back and your head held high, you project confidence and authority. This posture not only affects how the audience perceives you but can also influence how you feel about yourself, boosting your own confidence as you speak.

The use of gestures is another powerful tool in body language. Gestures can help emphasize points and add energy to your delivery. When using gestures, they should be purposeful and related to what you are speaking about. For example, enumerating points on your fingers can help the audience track with your arguments or highlighting something by pointing can draw attention to it. However, it's important to keep gestures natural and not overdo them, as too much gesturing can be distracting.

Facial expressions are equally important. Your facial expressions should match the tone of your message. If you are talking about something positive or exciting, your face should reflect enthusiasm or happiness. Conversely, a serious topic should have a more sober expression. Consistency between your expression and your words enhances the authenticity of your message and helps to convey your emotions effectively, making your speech more engaging.

Eye contact is a critical element of effective body language. Maintaining eye contact with your audience helps to create a connection and makes your listeners feel acknowledged. It shows that you are confident and sincere about your message. Try to make eye contact with different parts of the audience throughout your speech, rather than just focusing on a single point or person.

Moving around the stage can also be a useful body language technique, provided it is done with purpose. Walking from one side of the stage to the other can be used to transition between topics or to engage different parts of the audience. However, like gestures, movement should not be excessive. Aimless or continuous pacing can distract the audience from the message you are trying to convey.

The way you handle props or notes during a speech also plays a part in your body language. Holding notes tightly or fiddling with pens or other objects can convey nervousness. It is better to use notes minimally and keep your hands free as much as possible. If you do use notes, glance down at them quickly and maintain your connection with the audience as much as you can.

Practicing your body language is as important as practicing your speech. Record yourself delivering a speech or practice in front of a mirror. Pay attention to your posture, gestures, facial expressions, eye contact, and movement. This will allow you to see what you are doing well and what might need improvement.

In addition to self-review, feedback from others can be invaluable. Perform in front of friends or colleagues and ask for their honest feedback on your body language. They may notice things that you do not and can provide insights into how your non-verbal cues might be perceived.

Body language is a key component of effective public speaking. By mastering posture, gestures, facial expressions, eye contact, and movement, you can significantly enhance the effectiveness of your message. Remember, communication is not only about what you say but also about how you say it. Your body language can reinforce your words, making your message clearer and more memorable. By practicing and receiving feedback on your body language, you can become a more confident and compelling speaker.

❧❧❧

Engaging Your Audience: "Engagement isn't just about keeping attention, it's about sparking connection. Ask questions, invite responses, and interact with your audience as if having a conversation. The more involved your audience is, the more impactful your message will be. Engagement is the secret to turning listeners into believers. Let every speech be a two-way street."

❦❦❦

TWELVE

ENGAGING YOUR AUDIENCE

Engaging your audience is a critical aspect of successful public speaking. An engaged audience is attentive, responsive, and much more likely to be influenced by your message. Keeping an audience interested throughout a speech requires a combination of preparation, skill, and sensitivity to the crowd's reactions. Here are some effective methods to ensure your audience remains engaged from start to finish.

The first method to engage your audience is to start strong. The opening of your speech should capture the audience's attention immediately. You could start with a surprising statistic, a provocative question, a compelling story, or a humorous anecdote. Whatever your choice, make sure it is relevant to your main topic and sparks curiosity. A strong start sets the tone for the rest of your speech and can make the audience eager to hear what you will say next.

Once you have their attention, maintaining interest is the next challenge. One effective way to do this is by making your content relatable. Connect your topic to the experiences, interests, and concerns of your audience. When people see the relevance of what you're discussing to their own lives, they are more likely to pay attention and engage with the content. To achieve this, you need to know your audience well—understanding who they are, what matters to them, and why they are listening to your speech.

Variety in delivery is also crucial for keeping the audience engaged. Monotony can cause attention to wane, so mix up your speech with different elements. Alternate between stories, facts, rhetorical questions, and visuals. Change your tone and pace at different points to suit the content. For instance, speak faster to convey excitement and slow down to emphasize important points. These changes help keep the auditory experience interesting and prevent the audience from tuning out.

Interaction is another powerful tool to engage your audience. Encourage participation through direct questions, polls, or inviting audience members to share their experiences or opinions. Interaction not only makes the speech more dynamic but also gives the audience a sense of being part of the conversation. This can increase their investment in the topic and their attention to your words.

Using visuals can also help maintain interest. Visual aids like slides, charts, and videos can provide a break from listening and give the audience something engaging to look at. Ensure that any visual aids are clear, professional, and directly relevant to the content being discussed. They should serve as enhancements to your speech, not distractions.

Storytelling throughout your speech can also be a very effective way to keep the audience engaged. Stories allow people to connect emotionally with the message and can make complex information more digestible and memorable. Incorporate stories that illustrate your points in a vivid and meaningful way.

Another important aspect is to be aware of your audience's feedback and adapt accordingly. Watch for signs of engagement or disinterest. Are they nodding, smiling, or looking confused? Adapt your speech based on their non-verbal cues. If you notice a drop in energy or attention, you might need to inject a quick interactive element or a humorous remark to re-engage them.

Finally, close with a strong conclusion that reinforces your main message and leaves a lasting impression. Summarize key points briefly and end on a high note, whether it's a call to action, a thought-provoking question, or a powerful statement. A compelling closure can energize your audience and leave them thinking about your speech long after it's done.

Engaging your audience is essential for effective public speaking. By starting strong, making your content relatable, varying your delivery, interacting with the audience, using visuals effectively, incorporating storytelling, responding to audience cues, and ending with a powerful conclusion, you can keep your audience interested and responsive throughout your speech. These techniques will help ensure that your message not only reaches but also resonates with your listeners.

ᗆᗆᗆ

Handling Questions and Feedback: "Feedback is the mirror that reflects your effectiveness. Welcome it, embrace it, and grow from it. Questions are opportunities to extend your message and clarify your thoughts. Handle them with care, respect, and openness. Let your audience's curiosity inspire deeper insights."

ᗡᗡᗡ

THIRTEEN

HANDLING QUESTIONS AND FEEDBACK

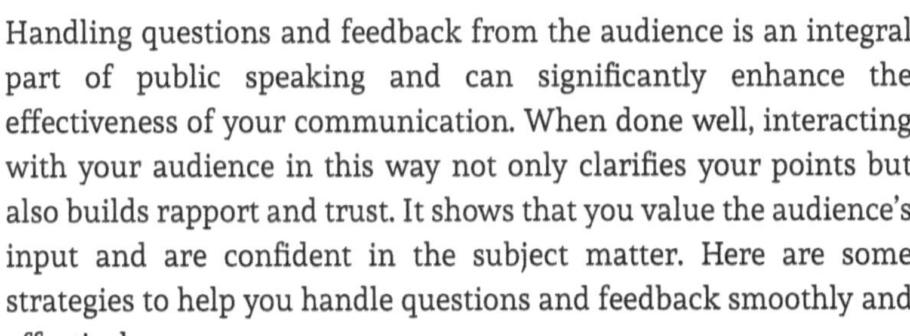

Handling questions and feedback from the audience is an integral part of public speaking and can significantly enhance the effectiveness of your communication. When done well, interacting with your audience in this way not only clarifies your points but also builds rapport and trust. It shows that you value the audience's input and are confident in the subject matter. Here are some strategies to help you handle questions and feedback smoothly and effectively.

First, it's important to foster an environment where your audience feels comfortable asking questions or providing feedback. Early in your speech, encourage them to hold their questions to the end or let them know if you prefer they ask questions as they arise. Your approach will depend on the format of your session and your comfort level. Either way, welcoming questions openly sets a positive tone for the interaction.

When you receive a question, listen attentively. This not only shows respect for the person asking but also ensures that you fully understand the question so you can respond appropriately. Avoid interrupting or finishing the question for them, even if you think you know what they are going to ask. Listening carefully also gives you a moment to formulate your response.

Once the question is asked, acknowledge the questioner. This can be as simple as a nod, or a verbal acknowledgment like "That's a great question." Such responses validate the questioner's effort to engage with your presentation. It's important to maintain a positive and open demeanor, even if the question is critical or challenging. Showing defensiveness or annoyance can alienate your audience and detract from your message.

When responding, be clear and to the point. If the question is complex, break down your answer into manageable parts. If you don't know the answer, it's perfectly acceptable to say so. You can respond with "I don't have that information right now, but I can find out and get back to you," or "That's an interesting question, I'll need to look into it further." Honesty in such situations helps maintain your credibility.

If the question is off-topic, gently steer it back to the relevant subject. You can say something like, "That's an interesting point, although it's a bit beyond the scope of this presentation. Let's discuss this afterward, or I can point you to some resources that address your question."

Managing feedback, particularly if it is critical, requires tact and professionalism. Listen to the feedback without interrupting, and acknowledge the person's perspective. You can say, "Thank you for sharing your thoughts. I appreciate your perspective." If the feedback is useful, express how it will influence your work or your thinking. If you disagree with the feedback, you can express this diplomatically by saying, "I see it differently, and here's why..." and provide reasons or evidence to support your viewpoint.

It's also beneficial to prepare for common questions or criticisms in advance. If there are aspects of your topic that are often misunderstood or controversial, prepare clear, concise responses. This preparation can help you respond with confidence and maintain control of the discussion.

During the question and answer session, maintain control of the time. If the questions are numerous or detailed, it's okay to limit the number of questions you take during the session. You can say, "We have time for two more questions," and offer to speak with people individually after the presentation if they have further questions.

Effectively handling questions and feedback is crucial for successful public speaking. By creating a welcoming atmosphere, listening carefully, acknowledging the audience's input, responding clearly, and managing critical feedback with professionalism, you can enhance your interaction with the audience. These practices not only make the session more informative and engaging but also strengthen your credibility and the impact of your presentation.

❦❦❦

The Role of Humor: "Humor breaks barriers and builds bridges. It lightens the load and enlightens the message. Use humor to heal, not hurt; to clarify, not confuse. A laugh can be just as powerful as a profound thought when delivered properly. Let humor illuminate your message, not overshadow it."

⊳⊳⊳

FOURTEEN

THE ROLE OF HUMOR

Humor is a powerful tool in public speaking that can lighten the mood, engage the audience, and create a memorable experience. When used effectively, humor can help break down barriers, making the audience more receptive to your message. It can also serve as a means of connecting with the audience on a personal level, fostering a sense of camaraderie and goodwill. However, using humor appropriately requires careful consideration of the context, the audience, and the timing.

One of the key benefits of incorporating humor into your speeches is its ability to relieve tension. Both the speaker and the audience can feel nervous at the outset of a presentation, and a well-timed joke or amusing anecdote can help to relax everyone. When people laugh, they release endorphins, which are natural stress-relievers. This not only improves the atmosphere but also makes the audience more open to listening and engaging with the content of your speech.

Understanding your audience is crucial when deciding to use humor. What is funny to one group may not be funny, or could even be offensive, to another. Consider the cultural, demographic, and professional backgrounds of your audience members. Humor that works well with young tech professionals may not resonate in the same way with retirees or educators. Doing a bit of research on your audience beforehand can help you tailor your humor to their interests and sensibilities.

The type of event can also determine the appropriateness of using humor. While a light-hearted talk at a conference might welcome some humor, a solemn occasion or a formal corporate presentation might require a more subdued approach. Always align your use of humor with the tone and purpose of the event.

When using humor, it is important to keep it relevant to the topic of your speech. Random jokes that do not tie into your message can distract the audience and detract from your credibility. Instead, use humor that enhances or illustrates your points. For example, if you are talking about overcoming challenges, you might share a humorous personal anecdote about a time when things didn't go as planned, but you learned a valuable lesson.

It's also advisable to keep the humor light and inclusive. Avoid controversial topics such as politics, religion, or anything that might be considered offensive. The goal is to make your audience laugh with you, not to make them feel uncomfortable or alienated.

Timing is another critical aspect of using humor effectively. Inserting humor at the beginning of a speech can be a great way to capture the audience's attention and set a friendly tone. Humor can also be effectively used as a transition between sections of your speech, helping to keep the energy up and ensuring that the audience remains engaged.

Self-deprecating humor can be particularly effective, as it shows your humility and makes you more relatable to your audience. However, it's important to strike the right balance so that it doesn't undermine your authority or the seriousness of your message.

Finally, practice is key to delivering humor effectively. What may seem funny in your head can fall flat in delivery if not practiced. Try out your humorous parts on friends or colleagues beforehand to gauge their reactions. This can help you refine your timing and delivery.

Humor can be a valuable element in public speaking when used appropriately. It can lighten the mood, enhance connections with the audience, and make your message more memorable. By understanding your audience, keeping the humor relevant and appropriate, and practicing your delivery, you can effectively integrate humor into your speeches and ensure it serves to support your overall message.

❦❦❦

Practicing Your Speech: "Practice transforms potential into performance. Rehearse not until you get it right, but until you can't get it wrong. Every practice session is a rehearsal for success. Own your words, feel them, live them before you speak them. The best speeches are lived before they are given."

❧❧❧

FIFTEEN

PRACTICING YOUR SPEECH

Practicing your speech is a critical step in the process of public speaking that cannot be overlooked. Effective rehearsal enhances your delivery, builds your confidence, and ensures that your message is communicated clearly and impactfully. Understanding the importance of practicing your speech and knowing how to do it effectively are key skills that every speaker should develop.

The first reason to practice your speech is to refine your delivery. During rehearsal, you can experiment with different tones, paces, and emphases to find the most effective way to convey your message. You can identify the best places to pause for effect, to change your tone to draw attention to a key point, or to adjust your volume to engage your audience. Each aspect of your delivery can be fine-tuned through repeated practice.

Another crucial aspect of practicing is to ensure familiarity with your material. Knowing your content well allows you to speak more naturally and fluidly without having to rely heavily on notes. This familiarity not only makes you look more knowledgeable and confident but also makes it easier to recover smoothly if you lose your place or get interrupted. The more you practice, the more instinctive your speech becomes, allowing you to focus more on engaging with your audience rather than recalling your next line.

Practicing also helps to reduce anxiety and build confidence. Public speaking can be nerve-wracking, and the fear of making mistakes in front of an audience can be daunting. Repeated rehearsals familiarize you with the act of delivering your speech, which can make the actual event feel less intimidating. Each time you practice, you reinforce your ability to perform, which naturally builds confidence.

To practice effectively, start by breaking down your speech into manageable segments. Focus on one segment at a time, perfecting each before moving on to the next. This approach allows you to pay close attention to the details of each part of your speech, such as the introduction, key points, transitions, and conclusion. It also helps in memorizing the content, as breaking it down into sections can make the overall speech less overwhelming.

Use a variety of practice methods. Practicing alone in front of a mirror can be effective for watching your body language and facial expressions. Recording your practice sessions and playing them back can help you hear your voice as others hear it, allowing you to notice and correct issues with volume, clarity, or intonation. Practicing in front of friends, family, or colleagues can provide you with valuable feedback from a listener's perspective.

During rehearsal, pay attention to timing. Use a timer to ensure that your speech fits within the allotted time. This is especially important if you are speaking at an event with strict time constraints. Knowing that your speech fits well within the given time can reduce anxiety and help you pace yourself correctly during the actual presentation.

As you get closer to the day of the event, try to simulate the speaking conditions as closely as possible. Practice in the clothes you will wear, use the same equipment you will use during the speech, and if possible, rehearse in the actual venue. This can help you feel more comfortable and prepared when it comes time to deliver the speech.

Lastly, incorporate any feedback you receive into your practice. Constructive criticism is invaluable, as it provides a fresh perspective on your speech and can highlight issues you might not have noticed. Use this feedback to make necessary adjustments and continue to refine your speech.

Practicing your speech is essential for effective public speaking. It allows you to refine your delivery, familiarize yourself with your material, reduce anxiety, and build confidence. By breaking your speech into segments, using various practice methods, paying attention to timing, simulating actual conditions, and incorporating feedback, you can ensure that your practice sessions are productive and lead to a successful and impactful presentation.

ppp

Adapting to Different Settings: "Flexibility is the hallmark of an effective speaker. Tailor your tone, content, and delivery to fit the setting and audience. The best speakers flow like water—adapting, adjusting, and accommodating. Understand the environment, and let it shape your speech, not constrain it. Speak to suit, not to fit."

ᐁᐁᐁ

SIXTEEN

ADAPTING TO DIFFERENT SETTINGS

Adapting your speech to different settings and contexts is a critical skill for any effective speaker. Whether you are presenting in a small meeting room, at a large conference, or even virtually, the ability to tailor your message and delivery to suit the venue and audience can significantly impact the effectiveness of your communication. Understanding how to modify your speech based on various factors ensures that your message is not only heard but also resonates with those listening.

The first step in adapting your speech is to understand the context of your presentation. Each setting has its own unique characteristics and challenges. For instance, speaking in a large auditorium requires a different approach than presenting in a cozy seminar room. In larger venues, your voice, gestures, and visual aids need to be bigger and more pronounced to reach and engage your entire audience. Conversely, in smaller settings, a more conversational tone and subtler gestures can be more effective.

Understanding your audience is just as crucial. Different audiences may have different expectations, knowledge levels, and interests. For example, a group of industry experts might require less background information but more detailed technical data than a general audience. Similarly, a corporate audience might expect a more formal presentation style compared to a casual community meeting. Tailoring your speech to meet the specific needs and expectations of your audience is key to ensuring that your message is effective.

Cultural considerations are also important when adapting your speech. Different cultures communicate and receive information in different ways. Some cultures value direct and straightforward communication, while others prefer a more nuanced or indirect approach. Being aware of these cultural differences and incorporating them into your speech can help in making your presentation more effective and respectful to the audience's norms.

Technology and equipment availability at the venue can also affect how you adapt your speech. For instance, if advanced multimedia tools are available, you might incorporate more video or audio elements into your presentation. On the other hand, if you're in a setting with limited technological support, you might need to rely more on your spoken words and physical presence to communicate your message.

Timing can also vary depending on the setting. In some contexts, you may have a full hour to delve deeply into your topic, while in others, you might only have a few minutes to convey your key points. Adjusting the depth and breadth of your content to fit the time available is crucial. This might mean focusing on just the most important information in shorter talks or developing more comprehensive material for longer sessions.

Interaction with the audience can also be adapted to different settings. In smaller groups, you might be able to engage in more direct interaction, such as asking questions and encouraging a dialogue. In larger settings, interaction might be more challenging, but techniques such as polling the audience or encouraging social media engagement during or after the presentation can be effective.

Practicing your speech in a way that anticipates these adaptations is essential. Rehearse different versions of your presentation to feel comfortable making adjustments based on the actual conditions you encounter. This might mean having different lengths of your speech ready or being prepared to skip certain sections if time is tight.

Adapting your speech for different settings and contexts is vital for effective public speaking. It involves understanding the unique characteristics of each venue and audience, incorporating cultural considerations, making use of available technology, adjusting to the allotted time, and planning for audience interaction. By carefully tailoring your presentation to suit these variables, you can ensure that your message is not only delivered effectively but also received positively by your audience. This adaptability not only enhances your credibility as a speaker but also maximizes the impact of your message.

ᗞᗞᗞ

Continuous Learning and Improvement: "The path of mastery in speaking is endless. Every speech is a lesson, every audience a teacher. Stay humble, stay curious, and stay committed to improvement. Growth is a choice—choose to evolve with every word you speak. Embrace each speaking opportunity as a stepping stone to greatness."

ᐅᐅᐅ

SEVENTEEN

CONTINUOUS LEARNING AND IMPROVEMENT

Continuous learning and improvement are fundamental for anyone who wishes to excel in public speaking. This ongoing process involves actively seeking feedback, engaging in self-reflection, and using these insights to enhance your skills. Understanding how to effectively utilize feedback and reflect on your experiences ensures that you keep growing as a speaker, allowing you to communicate more effectively and make a stronger impact on your audience.

Feedback is an invaluable tool for improvement. It provides external perspectives on your performance, highlighting both strengths and areas that need development. To benefit fully from feedback, it's crucial to seek it proactively from a variety of sources. After delivering a speech, ask your audience, colleagues, or a mentor to share their thoughts on how you did. Specific questions about your clarity, engagement, delivery, and content can guide them to provide detailed and constructive feedback.

However, receiving feedback is only part of the process; you must also learn how to accept and use it effectively. Listening to feedback can sometimes be challenging, especially if it is critical. It's important to approach feedback with an open mind and a positive attitude, seeing it as an opportunity to learn rather than a critique of your worth. Evaluate the feedback critically—consider what resonates with your own perceptions and what doesn't, and decide how to apply this information to improve your skills.

Self-reflection is another key component of continuous improvement. This involves taking the time after each speaking engagement to assess your own performance. Reflect on what went well and what didn't. Ask yourself what parts of the speech felt the most engaging and where you might have lost the audience's interest. Consider how your nerves, preparation, and interaction with the audience affected your delivery. Self-reflection helps you internalize both your successes and your mistakes, turning each speaking opportunity into a learning experience.

Setting specific, measurable goals based on feedback and self-reflection is an effective way to focus your improvement efforts. For example, if you receive feedback that your speeches are too detailed and hard to follow, you might set a goal to simplify your content and work on clearly defining your main points. Goals give you a clear direction for your practice sessions and help you measure your progress over time.

In addition to feedback and self-reflection, seeking out educational resources can further enhance your learning. There are numerous books, videos, workshops, and courses available on various aspects of public speaking. These resources can provide new techniques and insights that you can adapt and try out in your speeches. Learning from experts and observing how other successful speakers handle their presentations can inspire new approaches and ideas that you can incorporate into your own style.

Joining a speaking club or group, such as Toastmasters International, can also be beneficial. Such organizations provide a supportive environment where you can practice regularly, receive structured feedback, and observe a wide range of speaking styles. The continuous practice and community support found in these groups can significantly accelerate your learning and improvement.

Finally, incorporate the practice of mindfulness and awareness in your speaking. Being mindful of your speech patterns, body language, and audience reactions while speaking can help you make real-time adjustments to improve engagement. This awareness is crucial for mastering the art of public speaking and becoming adept at responding to the dynamic nature of live presentations.

Continuous learning and improvement in public speaking involve a cycle of seeking feedback, engaging in self-reflection, setting improvement goals, utilizing educational resources, and practicing mindfulness. By embracing this process, you can continually enhance your skills, adapt to new challenges, and grow as a speaker. This commitment to improvement not only boosts your confidence and effectiveness but also ensures that your audience always receives the best value from your presentations.

❦❦❦

Inspirational Case Studies: "Learn from those who've walked the path before you. Inspiration fuels our drive to achieve and exceed. Study great speakers—absorb their style, understand their substance, and tailor their techniques to your persona. Stand on the shoulders of giants, and you'll see further in your journey. Let their legacies light your way."

❥❥❥

EIGHTEEN

INSPIRATIONAL CASE STUDIES

Inspirational case studies of successful motivational speakers can provide valuable lessons for anyone looking to enhance their public speaking skills. By examining the journeys, techniques, and styles of renowned speakers, aspiring motivational speakers can gain insights into what makes an effective and impactful communicator. Here are a few examples of successful motivational speakers and key takeaways from their careers that can inspire and instruct others in the art of public speaking.

Tony Robbins is one of the most well-known motivational speakers in the world. His dynamic speaking style and ability to connect with audiences of thousands at his events have made him a prominent figure in the field of personal development. Robbins uses a combination of high energy, direct communication, and powerful storytelling to captivate and motivate his audience. His speeches often involve audience participation, physical activities, and personal anecdotes that relate to broader themes of overcoming adversity and achieving personal success. **Lesson:** Incorporating energy and interactivity can significantly enhance engagement and make the message more memorable.

Les Brown, another giant in the motivational speaking world, rose from humble beginnings to become one of the most sought-after speakers globally. Brown's key strength lies in his storytelling ability. He often shares his personal story of being labeled 'educable mentally retarded' in school to illustrate the power of belief and persistence. His authentic and heartfelt delivery resonates with many, making his messages of hope and resilience particularly impactful. **Lesson:** Authenticity and vulnerability in sharing personal stories can deeply connect with audiences and inspire them to action.

Brene Brown is a research professor who has spent her career studying courage, vulnerability, shame, and empathy. She became a global sensation after her TED talk on the power of vulnerability. Her ability to blend research with real-life stories makes her talks not only informative but also incredibly relatable. Brene's speaking style is conversational and inclusive, often using humor and self-deprecation to make her points. **Lesson:** Integrating research with personal stories and a touch of humor can make complex ideas accessible and engaging.

Simon Sinek is renowned for his concept of the "Golden Circle" and popularizing the idea of starting with 'why.' His TED talk on how great leaders inspire action is one of the most viewed talks online. Sinek uses simple graphics and clear, concise language to explain his ideas. His calm and deliberate speaking style helps him articulate his messages in a way that is easy to understand and compelling. **Lesson:** Clarity and simplicity in conveying complex concepts can help audiences grasp and remember your message.

Zig Ziglar, known for his warm, Southern charm and philosophical take on sales and personal development, was a master of the motivational quote. His ability to distill complex ideas into simple, memorable sayings was one of his most effective techniques. Ziglar's approach to motivational speaking was deeply rooted in values, integrity, and the importance of having a positive attitude. **Lesson:** Memorable, concise quotes can effectively reinforce your message and values.

Nick Vujicic was born without arms or legs but has turned his story into one of triumph over adversity. He speaks about his experiences and challenges to inspire others to overcome their own difficulties. His ability to connect with his audience through humor and honesty makes his messages of hope and resilience all the more powerful. **Lesson:** Demonstrating courage and humor in the face of adversity can inspire and uplift even in the most challenging circumstances.

By studying these inspirational case studies, aspiring speakers can learn valuable lessons in audience engagement, personal branding, and effective communication. Each of these speakers has unique strengths and styles, which underscores the importance of finding one's own voice and approach in the realm of public speaking. While techniques and styles can vary, the common thread among all successful motivational speakers is the ability to connect with their audience on a deep and meaningful level.

❧❧❧

Creating Your Personal Brand: "Your brand is your promise to your audience. It's what they expect from you and what you must deliver. Build it carefully, nurture it consistently, and present it confidently. Your personal brand is the reflection of your unique value. Make it memorable, make it impactful."

NINETEEN

CREATING YOUR PERSONAL BRAND

Creating a personal brand as a motivational speaker is crucial to establishing a unique identity that resonates with audiences and differentiates you in a competitive market. A strong personal brand reflects your values, beliefs, and the distinct message you want to convey through your speaking engagements. Here are some effective strategies for building a reputation as a motivational speaker that can help you connect with your intended audience and grow your professional career.

Firstly, it is important to define what you stand for. This involves deep self-reflection to understand your core values and the key messages you want to communicate. Consider what topics you are passionate about and how these relate to your personal experiences or professional expertise. This could be anything from overcoming adversity, pursuing personal development, enhancing productivity, or fostering positive workplace cultures. By focusing on a specific niche, you can hone your message and become known for your expertise in that area.

Once you have defined your niche, the next step is to develop a consistent message. Your public communications, whether through speeches, social media posts, blog articles, or podcasts, should consistently reflect your core message and values. Consistency helps reinforce your brand identity and makes you more memorable to your audience.

Building a professional website is also essential. Your website should serve as the central hub for your brand, showcasing your expertise, past speaking engagements, testimonials, and any relevant content you've created, such as blogs, videos, or podcasts. Ensure the website is professionally designed to reflect your brand image and is optimized for search engines to help potential clients find you easily.

Social media is a powerful tool for building and promoting your personal brand. Choose platforms that are most relevant to your target audience and regularly engage with them by sharing valuable content, interacting in discussions, and promoting your speaking events. Video content, such as short motivational clips or tips related to your speaking topics, can be particularly effective in engaging audiences and demonstrating your speaking style.

Networking is another key aspect of building your brand. Attend industry conferences, workshops, and other events where you can connect with potential clients and other speakers. These connections can lead to speaking opportunities, partnerships, and valuable endorsements. Don't underestimate the power of word of mouth; the more people who know about you and your speaking abilities, the more likely they are to recommend you to others.

Gathering and leveraging testimonials and case studies from past speaking engagements can significantly enhance your credibility. After each event, ask organizers and attendees for feedback. Positive testimonials can be used in your marketing materials, on your website, and on social media to show potential clients the impact of your work.

Another important strategy is to continually improve and update your speaking skills. The field of motivational speaking is dynamic, and audience expectations can change over time. Regularly invest in your professional development by attending speaker training sessions, hiring a coach, or learning from established speakers. This commitment to improvement not only makes you a better speaker but also demonstrates your dedication to your craft, which can be a strong part of your brand.

Finally, consider writing a book or articles on topics related to your speaking niche. Published works can greatly enhance your authority and visibility in your field. They provide another platform to solidify your expertise and reach a broader audience. Even starting with smaller publications or contributing to blogs in your industry can help build your reputation and visibility.

Building a personal brand as a motivational speaker involves a combination of defining your unique message, consistently promoting this message across multiple platforms, engaging with your audience, networking, gathering testimonials, continually improving your skills, and possibly authoring publications. By following these strategies, you can establish a strong, recognizable brand that resonates with audiences and opens up new professional opportunities.

ᐳᐳᐳ

Motivation is the silent whisper that urges you to keep going when the crowd has gone silent; it's the inner fire that burns brighter with each challenge faced. It transforms the daunting mountains of your doubts into stepping stones of success. Let this force guide you, for with motivation in your heart and determination in your steps, no goal is too distant, no dream too far-fetched.

ᚦᚦᚦ

TWENTY
NEXT STEPS

As we wrap up the exploration of the art of motivational speaking, it's important to reflect on the key points we've covered and consider the next steps to enhance your journey as a speaker. From understanding the basics of motivational speaking to adapting to different settings and continuously improving your skills, each component plays a crucial role in becoming an effective and impactful speaker.

First, we discussed the importance of understanding your audience and the power of empathy. Knowing who you are speaking to and connecting with them on an emotional level is foundational to motivational speaking. It ensures that your message resonates and has the desired impact.

Next, we delved into crafting your message with clarity and ensuring that it is both impactful and memorable. Using storytelling as a tool can greatly enhance the engagement and retention of your audience, making your message stick. We also emphasized the importance of being authentic and genuine in your delivery. Your audience can sense insincerity, and it can undermine even the most well-crafted messages.

Developing confidence and overcoming public speaking fears are also essential. Confidence allows you to deliver your message powerfully and persuasively, while managing fear ensures that your delivery is smooth and effective. Incorporating visual aids and mastering your vocal and body language techniques further supports this, enabling a more polished and professional presentation.

Engaging your audience and handling their responses effectively is key to interactive and dynamic speaking. Using humor appropriately can lighten the mood and make the content more digestible, while practicing your speech thoroughly prepares you for a confident delivery. Adapting your message to different settings and audiences enhances the relevance and impact of your talks, making your speeches more effective regardless of the context.

Continuous learning and improvement should be a constant in your career as a speaker. Seeking feedback, reflecting on your performances, and setting personal development goals are all crucial steps to refining your skills and expanding your expertise. Networking with other speakers and learning from their experiences can also provide valuable insights and opportunities.

As you move forward in your speaking journey, consider these next steps to continue growing and improving:

Set Specific Goals: Identify specific aspects of your speaking skills that you want to improve or new topics you wish to tackle. Setting goals gives you a clear direction and something tangible to work towards.

Seek Opportunities to Speak: Whether in smaller community settings or larger conferences, every opportunity to speak is an opportunity to improve. Seek out these chances actively and consider different formats, such as workshops or webinars, to expand your repertoire.

Invest in Professional Development: Consider taking courses, attending workshops, or getting a coach to help refine your skills and introduce you to new techniques and perspectives.

Gather and Utilize Feedback: Continuously seek feedback from your audiences and peers. Use this feedback constructively to make informed adjustments to your presentations.

Reflect Regularly: Set aside time to reflect on your speeches and the responses they generate. Reflection is a powerful tool for self-improvement and can help you understand what works well and what doesn't.

Expand Your Knowledge: Stay informed about the latest research and trends related to your topics of interest. This not only enhances your credibility but also ensures that your content remains relevant and up-to-date.

Write and Publish: Consider writing articles, blogs, or even a book related to your speaking topics. Publishing can enhance your credibility and broaden your impact beyond the stage.

The journey of a motivational speaker is one of continuous growth and adaptation. By focusing on these areas and embracing the process of learning and improvement, you can build a fulfilling career that not only inspires and motivates others but also brings personal satisfaction and growth. Remember, every speech is an opportunity to make a difference. Keep refining your craft, and you will continue to inspire and motivate your audiences effectively.

ᗽᗽᗽ

True motivation comes from within, a relentless calling that propels you forward even on the darkest days. It is not just the desire to achieve, but the refusal to accept failure as the final chapter. Harness this power, let it fuel your journey, and watch as ordinary paths unfold into extraordinary adventures.

ᛈᛈᛈ

TWENTY-ONE
SUMMARY

Throughout our exploration of motivational speaking, we have delved into various aspects that are crucial for anyone looking to inspire and influence others through the power of speech. Each component we've covered serves as a building block for becoming a successful motivational speaker. Here, we summarize the key points from each topic to provide a cohesive overview and practical guide.

Understanding your audience is the first critical step in motivational speaking. Knowing who you are speaking to allows you to tailor your message and delivery to meet their needs and expectations. This involves recognizing their backgrounds, values, and the challenges they face, which can significantly enhance the impact of your message.

Empathy is a powerful tool in connecting deeply with your audience. It involves more than understanding their feelings; it's about genuinely caring and showing that you are aligned with their emotions and experiences. This connection can make your speeches more relatable and impactful.

Crafting a clear and compelling message is essential. Clarity ensures that your audience can easily follow and grasp your message, while the power of storytelling helps to embed your points in the minds of your listeners. Using stories effectively can make your presentations not only engaging but also memorable.

Being authentic in your delivery shows your true self to the audience, which builds trust and credibility. Your authenticity encourages a genuine connection with your listeners, making your message more believable and persuasive.

Developing confidence and overcoming public speaking fears are necessary for delivering your message effectively. Confidence comes from thorough preparation and practice, while learning to manage fears ensures that you can speak with authority and calm, regardless of the size or nature of the audience.

Utilizing visual aids and mastering vocal and body language techniques can significantly enhance the delivery of your speech. Visual aids help to clarify and emphasize your points, while effective use of your voice and body language can engage and hold the audience's attention.

Engaging your audience throughout your presentation keeps them interested and interactive. This can be achieved through questioning, active participation, and responsive adjustments based on their cues. Handling audience interactions, such as questions and feedback, with respect and consideration shows that you value their input and engagement.

Injecting humor appropriately can lighten the mood and make the content more enjoyable, helping to break down barriers and making the information more digestible. However, it's important to use humor sensitively and appropriately, considering the context and audience demographics.

Practicing your speech is perhaps one of the most direct ways to improve your speaking skills. Regular rehearsal helps refine your delivery, makes you more familiar with your material, and builds confidence. Adapting your speech to different settings and contexts ensures that your message is always appropriate and impactful, regardless of where you are speaking or who you are speaking to.

Continuous learning and improvement are what sustain a long-term career in motivational speaking. Seeking feedback, engaging in self-reflection, and pursuing professional development opportunities are vital for keeping your skills sharp and your content relevant.

Creating a personal brand as a motivational speaker involves defining and consistently communicating your unique message and style. This helps establish your identity in the field and can open up more speaking opportunities. Building and maintaining a professional image through various platforms, including social media and a personal website, can enhance your visibility and reputation.

Becoming a successful motivational speaker is a multifaceted process that requires dedication to mastering the craft of speaking, understanding the audience, and continuously improving. By integrating these elements—audience understanding, empathy, message clarity, authenticity, confidence, visual and vocal techniques, engagement strategies, humor, practice, adaptability, and personal branding—you can become a motivational speaker who not only delivers speeches but inspires and transforms lives. Whether you are just starting or seeking to enhance your speaking career, focusing on these fundamentals will equip you with the tools to succeed and leave a lasting impact on your audiences.

ᑭᑭᑭ

Other Books Of The Author

1. Empowering Minds: A Journey into Women's Self-Discovery and Power
2. The Dynamics of Motivation: Catalyzing Thought into Action
3. Meditation and Mental Well Being: The Path to Inner Peace and Clarity
4. The Psychology of Child Education: Nurturing Future Generations
5. Ethical Enlightenment: A Modern Guide to Living with Integrity
6. Voices of Empowerment: Stories of Women Rising Against Odds
7. Social Psychology in Everyday Life: Understanding Human Connections
8. The Essence of Motivational Speaking: Inspiring Change in Others
9. Balancing Acts: Women, Work, and the Will to Lead
10. Guiding with Grace: Raising Children with Compassion and Awareness
11. The Power of Positive Aging: Embracing Life After Fifty
12. Building Resilient Communities: Social Work in Action
13. The Ethical Educator: Principles for Teaching and Learning
14. From Insight to Impact: Social Psychology for a Better World
15. The Ethics of Empathy: A Guide to Ethical Living
16. The Science of Empowering the Self: Navigating Life's Challenges with Psychological Wisdom
17. The Mindful Conscious Leader: Meditation Techniques for Modern Management
18. Pioneering Spirit: Women's Pathways to Leadership and Empowerment
19. Feeling to Healing: The Role of Emotional Intelligence in Child Development
20. Transformative Talks and Words of Inspiration: Insights into Motivational Oratory

21. Green Ethics: A Path to Sustainable Living
22. Spiritual Integrity: Navigating Life with Moral Compassion
23. Clean Living, Clean Society: The Ethics of Cleanliness
24. Patriotic Spirits: Building a Nation on Positive Attitudes
25. Innovative Integrity & Vibrant Visions: The Ethical and Entrepreneurial Spirit of Gujarat
26. Youthful Visions, Endless Possibilities: Inspiring Ethics and Motivation in Children
27. Living Your Legacy: How to Motivate Others by Living Your Values
28. Secret of Healing Conversations: Ethical Practices in Counselling and Therapy
29. Creative Kindness: Crafting a Life of Compassion and Creativity
30. The Power of Appreciation: How Gratitude Can Transform Your Relationships
31. Bhagavad-Gita: Messages
32. Science of Art: The New Frontier of Fashion Modernism
33. Vivekananda's Virtues: A Blueprint for Modern Living
34. Empower Her: Navigating the Path to Women's Entrepreneurship
35. The Boundless Classroom: Innovations in Global Education
36. The Language of Leadership: Communicating with Authenticity and Impact
37. The Warrior's Mantra: Deciphering the Hanuman Chalisa
38. Echoes of Empathy: Transformative Stories of Social Service
39. Artful Living: Cultivating Creativity in Your Daily Routine
40. Finding Your Why: Discovering Your Passions and Charting Your Course
41. The Role of Social Media in Shaping Self-Esteem and Interpersonal Relationships among Adolescents

ॐॐॐ

Citation And References

This book represents the culmination of extensive research and meticulous analysis, incorporating a diverse range of sources, including numerous books, scholarly studies, and personal experiences. Additionally, I have scoured various websites to gather relevant information and data essential for the compilation of this work. I have taken every precaution to ensure the accuracy of the information presented and have diligently cited all sources to acknowledge their contributions.

Despite these efforts, the possibility of inadvertent errors remains. I deeply value the insights of my readers and appreciate any feedback that can help identify and rectify such inaccuracies. I encourage you to bring any discrepancies to my attention.

Your feedback is not only welcome but crucial, as it will aid in correcting current editions and enhancing the content of future ones. I am committed to maintaining the highest standards of accuracy and reliability in my work and thank you for your support and understanding.

Additionally, I firmly uphold the principle of freedom of speech and expression as guaranteed under Article 19(1)(a) of the Constitution of India, and I respect the diverse viewpoints and expressions of all readers.

ppp

Contact

Dr. Minakshi Bansal
Social Activist
Ahmedabad, Gujarat, Bharat
minakshiindiag20@yahoo.com

ೢೢೢ

|| LOKAHA SAMASTHAHA SUKHINO BHAVANTU ||

❦❦❦